Warrior
For Peace

STEVE
MASON

A TOUCHSTONE BOOK
Published by Simon & Schuster Inc.
NEW YORK · LONDON · TORONTO · SYDNEY · TOKYO

Copyright © 1988 by Steve Mason
All rights reserved
including the right of reproduction
in whole or in part in any form
Published by the Simon & Schuster Trade Division
Simon & Schuster Building
Rockefeller Center
1230 Avenue of the Americas
New York, New York 10020
TOUCHSTONE and colophon are registered trademarks
of Simon & Schuster Inc.

Designed by Deirdre C. Amthor

Manufactured in the United States of America
10 9 8 7 6 5 4 3 2 1 Pbk.
Library of Congress Cataloging in Publication Data
Mason, Steve.
    Warrior for peace / Steve Mason.
        p.   cm. — (A Touchstone Book)
    ISBN 0–671–66384–4 Pbk.
    1. Vietnamese Conflict, 1961–1975—Poetry.   I. Title.
PS2563.A798W3   1988   88–1585
811'.54—dc 19   CIP

Dedicated to

GEORGE HARRIS II

In time of war, a U.S. Marine;
in truth, a man of peace—
either way, a man of courage.

CONTENTS

INTRODUCTION

The first time I heard of Steve Mason, at a Vietnam Veterans of America reunion in Washington in August of '87, he got up on the podium and to a roomful of hundreds of hard-eyed vets, some in uniform, some not, some believing in what we had fought for over there and some not, he had the audacity to speak a poem—his poem—"Johnny's Song"—it's getting more and more famous among vets. I'd never heard it, but when I did it chilled me to a bone I thought would never again be touched by poetry. It cut through the room—without bullshit or pomposity which mark for me a lot of what I don't like about poetry—and stilled for a moment the heart of the civil war division in this country between the left and the right so evident in that roomful of veterans, and cut through to the pure thick muscle of beauty on a human tongue—albeit a hard-boiled Brooklyn staccato with pavement phrasing—but a voice unique of a goddamn walking-around Poet—in the true barbaric meaning of the word—a bard, a prophet crying out in the wilderness, our Homer come home to remember us (to make us not forget) the ten *fucking* years the Trojan Wars ate us *and* this country up the ass:

In my sad past
when I was still young,
I came home from war, alone;
my soul an unhung murderer.

One dark night
it stepped heavily on the trapdoor of my guilt
and decorously hanged itself.

I pray it has found peace
away from me.
Perhaps, even now
it is grandfather
to the unborn dreams
of several particular rice farmers
I knew years ago
(and killed before I ever met).

These days,
the rest of me
is less agreeable
to romance and to war.
I am hard at work
making tomorrow come true
for the children
who have (thus far) survived.

I am a warrior for peace.
And not a gentle man.

Or the Odyssean overtones of his poem to coming home—"To Brooklyn, with Love":

The first time I was born
was as an American.
The last time
was as a Human Being.
. . . .
Brooklyn was long before Vietnam.
All American men my age
suffered the bad luck and ill-timing
of drawing Vietnam and women's lib
in the same ten years!

Sort of like getting hit by a truck
the same day they told you
about the stomach cancer.

Sure, we were prepared for a world
that no longer existed.
Sure, we were this nation's
last generation of heroes—
unburied dinosaurs,
extinct only in our lack of purpose.

Our nation would honor us
(if only it could, posthumously).
It ignored us instead.

Or the wrath:

> On all sides of the issues
> on both sides of any ocean,
> veterans mistrust anyone in a position to lie:
> Wives, girlfriends, government officials,
> salesmen, lawyers, and the rich.

> Veterans trust dogs,
> children under twelve,
> masturbation,
> the chair facing the door
> and any weapon in the dark.

And finally the healing forgiveness and lilting sing-song beauty of "A Living Memorial":

> If there is a heaven
> a lifetime before Death,
> surely, it is a simple place
> where men such as we,
> who have earned the right
> to call each other brother,
> and women, such as you,
> who grace our lives,
> would come and stand together
> in the common truth of our world
> and learn there, a human language
> in which we would speak of peace
> to the children who bless our lives.

Here then is a warrior for peace, a Poet whose poems will last if we last, a prophet crying out to an America marching on a new self-imposed path to war. May the flinty weapons of Mind, Word and Love shine through the black depths of Madness and Death without Meaning. America wake up! No more Empire. No more Third World border wars. No more Vietnams.

Oliver Stone
November, 1987
Santa Monica, California

Warrior
For Peace

THIS TIME, A WARRIOR FOR PEACE

Somewhere,
in the sad past
of each man alone,
is a woman
a song
a war
which if put to music
would be strings and harp,
symbols and cannon
for Maestro Toscanini
orchestrating spring
in each man's soul.

There,
seated in the balcony
of each man's sense
of what might have been,
is the memory
of a young man
with sad eyes,
hearing "no"
from a lover
who would have made
all the difference.

Now,
(music aside)
he huffs and puffs
in the middle-aged city
of his choking dreams,
pulling on a waistline
too big for Levi's
and sees life through eyes
the color of faded denim—
sandpapered smooth as water
by the truth of her absence.

Tomorrow waits;
a buzzard on a signpost
with his name . . .

One street over, maybe,
he might have lived, who knows?
Forever? And why not?
With a girl who fit
as tight as his imagination,
never got a head cold
or had a daughter
who needed braces.

And he wonders this fine day,
sitting on a spiritual knoll
somewhere on the bright side
of Venus
(and the dark side of youth)
just how far behind him
was that promise
of what might have been.
And what if he refused to budge
a galactic inch from here & now?

Could her Time catch up
on some parabolic line
from when they first said hello?
And would she this time say "yes"?

Ah, who knows how many tries
a happy man has had at life?

It is possible that each man's song
travels across the universe
like a musical rainbow,
arched in the harmonics of joy,
calling the cosmic matter
of his unborn children.

Well,
when with what years bring,
this poet goes the way of all dreams,
his song will still travel
until mathematics are displaced
by providence.
And still I will wait. And I will call.
And I will wonder.
But not of her.
And not of my children.

I will wonder of war.
And of the sons and daughters
of my enemy
whose real and separate worlds I broke;
ultimately and infinitely
in the rude finality of senseless Death.

When we kill a dreamer,
we bury alive
ten thousand dreams
and all his unborn children.

In this age of nuclear weapons
there is not enough world
to dig so deep a hole.

Even now,
on nights too real for sleep,
I can feel the human voices
of those aborted dreams
from deep within me—
and far, far out there.

And so I speak with them,
"Do re me fa so la ti do."
And then, I do not move.
I do not breathe.
I lift my chin to heaven
and listen in my heart
to their music—
knowing it will never,
never
be.
Oh, war. war. war.
There are casualties taken
on both sides of life.
We come from nonexistence.
We got to oblivion.
And war denies us
the middle worth living.

In my sad past
when I was still young,
I came home from war, alone;
my soul an unhung murderer.

One dark night
it stepped heavily
on the trapdoor of my guilt
and decorously hanged itself.

I pray it has found peace
away from me.
Perhaps, even now
it is grandfather
to the unborn dreams
of several particular rice farmers
I knew years ago
(and killed before I ever met).

These days,
the rest of me
is less agreeable
to romance and to war.
I am hard at work
making tomorrow come true
for the children
who have (thus far) survived.

I am a warrior for peace.
And not a gentle man.

SONNET FOR A DEAD BROTHER

Yuri Schevchenko. (I can't pronounce your name.)
We never met—might not have liked each other.
But you and I, dead sergeant, were much the same.
"Internationalist combatants," brother!
Strange, your family could not speak your glory;
and mine (with free speech) never spoke to my war.
Pravda did not mention where you died, Yuri,
nor the cause your grieving father lost you for.
"What nation," he asks, "and what good cause in time
lists the cost of any war in human terms?"
Governments do not record in human rhyme,
nor newspapers print simple truth from rice berms.

Afghans, Viet Cong, you, me, all the others—
we were all poor men, better met as brothers.

A FIFTH AND FINAL SEASON

If we were to permit behavior
to substitute for reason,
a dialogue might ensue
between humankind and all other forms of life;
each a part of it all.

If nature were to speak, therefore,
on behalf of cauliflower & mussels—
wind & rain, the opportunity of maggots
and the rising yeast of gingerbread men,
it would speak of the eloquent balance
of spring—in whose fragile speech
is the acceptance of Death
and in whose wise discussion of beauty
motherhood finds the perfection of its young.

Hope, a dauntless, diminutive fiddler,
whistles softly and follows slowly
the skittish trail of a garden snail.

Each of our young,
entering reality through the lips
of April's promise,
knows that life must die
that life might live.

Yet, only man kills
without a sense of rhythm.
It is the design flaw of the species
that owing to his flexibility,
it is he who must devour himself.

Born into this small, green world,
with an appetite precisely equal
to his own extinction,
mankind, unto himself,
becomes a force of nature.
He is the fifth and final season.

Where mankind will go
neither spring nor hope will follow.
Many of his gods will go with him.

A PERFECT PINK BELLY

And into this room
your full, proud face
rises like a white moon
over the rim of the crib.

It hangs (a swollen moment)
before falling
and drops like the smile
of a crazed evangelist
onto the perfect pink belly
of your perfect pink baby.

And your kisses are mad things.
Alive. With wet little minds
of their own.
Snorting, sniffling, giggling things—
intent on the mischief of pure joy . . .

Chrumpff! To the belly!!
Phrumph! Phrumph!! Hey! ChicgaChicga!!
To the soft, powdered underchin.
Much laughy sounds and a little spit-up.
Gosh, life is good!

Hey, Daddy! Hold it a second, will ya?
Lemme ask you somethin', big fella.
How do ya do it?

Play this loving night
with your sweet child
and in the morning
ask for war with your vote?
Cast your ballot
for isolation and destruction?

Ask that someone's older son go off to war
and stick another poor, loving father's son
in the middle of his still almost pink belly
until his intestines spill out his life
like somebody squeezed the guts
from a Japanese beetle?
And *his* father wails to the moon
like a wild creature whose god
has not yet been born?

How do you do it?
I'd really hate to know.
No shit.

SIMPLE WISHES

In Tijuana, surely.
Maybe, on a hillock
in "Cardboard City."
Two children die slowly
and are dead, finally
of starvation.
No more questions in their eyes.

He who was their father
sinks into the mud of his shame.
He rises (somehow) later
empty into his rage.

Across the no-man's-land
of barbed wire and national borders
(a distance beyond geography)
the lights of San Diego dance
to the rhythm and the promise
of high-tech immortality.

Before Dawn,
before God,
before life (really) begins,
forty thousand boys and girls
(from everywhere and nowhere)
will die
before our very open mouths.
(Never) any questions in our eyes.

Each night,
every day,
they give up the need
for a 2¢ bowl of rice
or a 6¢ vaccination for measles.
Or a priceless drink
of untainted water
which doesn't drain their guts
into the sand.
Or into the gutter.

Strange, even in the end,
the little ones never give up dreams.
How gentle must be God's hand
to pry such small fingers
from such simple wishes.

DEATH IS A LADY

Six or seven thousand mornings ago,
somewhere along a scary border, in bad times,
a Cambodian mercenary at my side,
said, in his tongue, to no one in particular,
"Death is a Lady."

Something like two hundred seconds later
(each sharp enough to split an atom)
the Cambot lay dead (his boots at odd angles).

I, smoking what I thought was my last Pall Mall,
looked past him through the much heavier smoke
and saw the face of God
(something like jelly dripping from His mouth).

CBS News did not carry the events of our day.
Not too many knew at the time, and none care today,
that my buck-toothed friend with the bowed legs
played soccer with courage and pride and grace
for the Cambodian National Team in the '52 Olympics.

Nobody cared at the time and few care today
that I decided never to war in another jungle—
and to take the fight into the streets as a poet.

I do not know to what grand dispersal
my friend has gone or what he does there,
but I quit smoking and I'm trying to write.

Death may be a lady,
but God is no gentleman.

A LIVING MEMORIAL

If there is a heaven
a lifetime before Death,
surely, it is a simple place
where men such as we,
who have earned the right
to call each other brother,
and women, such as you,
who grace our lives,
would come and stand together
in the common truth of our world
and learn there, a human language
in which we would speak of peace
to the children who bless our lives.

It is the courage of America
and the strength of our world
that the essence of our patriotism
is not nationalism,
it is humanity.

Therefore, we will survive together—
all our good and natural intentions
realized in quick, evolving thrusts
from chance to choice,
from random twitches at self-determination,
to deliberate, articulate commitments.
Generation to generation.

And there will come one fine day
when the best and the brightest of us
will be men and women dedicated to tolerance.
Human beings all, not willing
to be the posthumous heroes of their time—
deceased for country and for transient cause.

These will be the living heroes
of our final victory.
Warriors for peace
who will live with human dignity
to serve conscience
and the nature of all life.

They will be those of us who know
the spirit of peace is brave compromise.
And the character of negotiation
is the value system of the community.

Until then,
it is not enough
to love our children
(the most human of ourselves).
We must respect their right
to inherit our only world
on the morning of some gentle tomorrow
encouraged with their joy.

Until then, we must teach them
what they already know—
there is no victory
other than in balance.

From such
is all we can pray for today
and all we will ever come to know
of forever.

HINT OF DEATH

There is no crime in nature.
There is only struggle.
Survival is the action of life;
it is done without explanation.

In nature,
personal failure is death.
Group failure is extinction.
Life is; or it is not.

There is no beauty in nature—
there is no apology; only balance.
Simplicity approaches perfection.
It is so.

Civilization is *un*natural.
It is mankind walking off the grass.
He sits his nature on new concrete
and waits at the curb of his cities
for a word of the advancing peace.

There is gunfire in the side streets.
Hunger is the bedtime story of children.
Microchips bring news of free lunches.
Electric churches flash the word of man.
His air escapes from a hole in the roof.

Man's written laws become his government.
Natural people (in an illiterate world)
obey unread rules which limit their options
and encourage the survival of the writers.

Whatever his concept of the universe,
in whichever force of nature his soul confides,
each man knows in his teeth, the laws of man
cannot modify the laws of his own nature.
Natural law is the true word of his only god.

In limitation there is the hint of Death.

NEW BROOM

One elegant morning
we will see the wind
dressed up in a light-
green phosphorescence,
wearing a palm tree
behind its left ear.

Between
its hissing lips
stained the color
of sweet cherries,
scattered children
will tongue the streets.

On that final day,
someone among us
will say to no one,
"Oops!"

And then
be swallowed cleanly
by a new broom
sweeping the world
of its latest mistake. . . .

ONLY ONE MOTHER

There is only one mother.

We call her many names—
reach out from separate sleeps
for her billion shapeless breasts
and as she bites her twisted lower lip
we squeeze her dry.

Still, we grope for her.
Still, even in her arms,
we cry for her—sense the truth
of her nonexistence.

What exists is our need only.
The singular need for the one
true mother of us all.

In that need, then,
there IS only one mother.

Just as there is only one war.

We scream
from under separate martial skies
for the earth mother's breast.
Later, under peacetime ceilings,
we bite deep
into the soft tit-edges
of midnight pillows
tossed from sleepless writhings
like rag dolls
onto the clawing space of lost battlegrounds.

But there is only one betrayal
of the one nation's perfect son.
Only the one war we fight over and over—
a baton-passing, father to son,
generation to generation, degeneration.

The ultimate child abuse.
The son is dead!
Long live the father!
(Mom, bursting with pride
and brimming with sacrifice.)

Mom. War.
We tattoo
our devotion
onto our hairy arms
and bony knuckles.
We brand deep
in the purple language
of our Time and Place
the twin adorations
of our hard manhood
into our tough hides
the names of our first "blood" loves
as if we are afraid to forget
whose property we are
and to what we belong,
as if where we come from
describes for what we will die
and for what, therefore,
our lives are all about.

Mother. War.
In these, we declare
our obedience
and bleed (a little more)
to prove our loyalty.

Mother. War.
Birth. Death.
Life is not personal.
Life feels personal.

It comes deeply to us
like a particulate
drawn into our lungs
on the social air
of our first conscious breathing,
that there is choice.
But there is none.
We breathed a lie—
real as a thread of cultural asbestos
lodged in our chests for a lifetime.
There IS no choice.

Nothing particularly personal.
Only the enculturation
and the biology.

Yet, we live
as if the greatest decisions of our lives
were the circumstance of our gestations
and the cumulative political debacles
of our entire generation.

The truth is,
we have no more say in our enemies of state
than we did in the selection of our mothers.

Between birth and death,
most good sons
have a wife or two or three
(looking for a mother they can Really love)
raise a few children
(stranding one or two)
and wade through several tons
of social excrement
wearing testicle-high value systems
and endless sports programming
as prophylactics against the responsibility
to be people (instead of simply men).

Life, it seems, can be sweet
if you don't notice it.

These days,
I've become something heavy,
something slow—
a jar of old pennies
(too numerous to count)
and anyway, too few to make a difference.

My war is over.
My mother is dead.
The kids are grown.
And the ink is dry
on the words I once believed.

There is only one life
just as there is only one death.
It is time, I think, to die
(from what I am)
to exchange myself
for a bright, new thing
some clever god might fashion
to serve a better end—
time to let some cosmic "mother"
change me into something special
which expands itself
and expends itself
that others may live a higher truth
and come to know
that illusive, natural balance
we call the one and only "peace."

I would go now (and gladly)
to be its champion.

Perhaps you could tell me
what else there is to do.
Or, maybe, you could join me on the way—
brothers and sisters, in the cause of peace.

Broken dreams are like deaths in the family
and being orphaned (at any age) is all alone.

OF MARGO AND THE BOYS

Strange,
we pay money to our soldiers
and fix their teeth.
We give them medals
when they kill for us.
We respect our boy children.
And we love them.

Margo (not her real name)
walks the streets,
an abscess in her jaw.
She'll do you favors—
make your dreams come true.
Margo makes love for a living.
We hate our Margos.
And we punish them.

We live in a world
whose system reveres power.
It is the ultimate virtue.
The takers of life
are the obedient servants
of the most powerful.

It is the passive of us
who are most ridiculed.
Our mothers and daughters
who are vilified and debased.

It is ironic
that when the war is over,
old soldiers with bad gums
learn too late whom they served.

TO BROOKLYN, WITH LOVE

The seventh man I knew I ever killed,
caught me with a mouthful of tuna.

At the time, I didn't see any reason
not to finish the sandwich,
but I've never forgiven myself
for not having the decency
to spit *that* bite out.

I thought of him on May 7, 1985,
the day of the New York City Parade
to "Welcome Home" America.

Thought of him like a slap to the face
when I stepped from the subway car
onto the elevated platform
about New Utrecht Avenue, Brooklyn.

I was born in Brooklyn
in the beginning of the war in Europe.
I was born again, sometime later,
in the middle of another war in Asia.

The first time I was born
was as an American.
The last time,
was as a Human Being.

Either way, this special day,
I was coming home.

To my country.
To the old neighborhood.
And to the house where I was born.

It was a gray, sometimes rainy day.
The kind when buildings and sky
and the faces of people
blend with Time itself
into a kind of oneness—
some kind of haunting,
shapeless thing, without color,
like a child's lump of clay
waiting in the attic to be discovered.

I stood at the end of the platform
(a foot on the railing)
and leaned out and into it—
this thing within myself—
that waited for me out there.

The small windows of Brooklyn apartments
were inset against the telephone lines
like black notes on sheet music.
One upon the other, my eye fell on them
like the armature of a music box.
And I watched the classic melody
of the Borough of Brooklyn
play behind my mind
like Debussy's Claire de Lune—
just like my father played it,
one stop closer to Coney Island,
a lifetime before mine
(when the century was new)

and he was just another Italian kid
growing up in the New World.
A stealer of apples.
A player of punchball.
Of stoopball.
And of the violin.

The proof of those times
was not on the streets,
nor in the houses.
It was (and is) in my blood.

A liquid menagerie of pulsing moments
shared by parents when I was young.
And more violently,
by the steel-hard traumas of their lives
injected into my grooved veins
like congenital pinballs
bruising straight for my brain—
lit for "replay" with the pounding
ding-ding, ding-ding of synchronicity.

Today, this time, this place
would light my inside-outside world
with the bumper bonus
of three generations
(on both sides of the family).
Brooklynites, all.

I left the platform
and found the street level—
absently, like a suicide
hits the law of gravity. Hard.

Like the coming to all facts is hard.
(Truth comes more slowly to our lives.)

I stood there flat-footed
on the naked, wet fact
that I was standing on a Brooklyn street
in the spring of 1985
emotionally dissolving
in and of myself
and that when I had hit the street level
I had come to stand squarely in my past.

I shuffled toward home
(a reluctant negotiation).
Feet caught in an undertow
of four decades
pulling at the reality of my calendar.

Memory argued with reason.
Store fronts and curbs wavered
between Then and Now—
flat memories surfaced to the street
like dead flounder.
And I began to remember.

. . . The war with Germany
was coming to a close
about the time I hit the streets as a boy.

Those were the Lash LaRue,
penny-candy days
of singing lariats, cast-iron cap guns
and all-day matinees.

I don't know who it was
who designed the silver handles
on the Good Humor truck,
but the guy who came up
with the Saturday matinee
was a genius!

Movies. Serials. Cartoons.
All in a theater so dark,
so fun, so delicious
we'd emerge hours later—
blinking, disoriented,
giggling psychotics
who shielded our eyes
from the reality of Brooklyn
like we were molemen
up from a deep hole
for a quick look-see.

And do you remember those bag lunches?!
Mashed egg sandwiches (made with love)
hard-boiled eggs
(wrapped in Cut-Rite wax paper)
a whack of salami, some carrot sticks,
enough Yankee Doodle cupcakes
to withstand a biblical famine,
and then (and THEN) the candy counter!
Geez!!

How come? How come we got so much food?
How come most of us
from the old neighborhood to this day
spell love F O O D?

Because in those days food was scarce
and sacrificing for kids
was a way of life. A philosophy.

But mostly, because the mothers
(and grandmothers)
who prepared those huge sacks
for us little kids
were refugee European women
born with a siege mentality
and a sense that each time
they said good-bye,
it might be the last.

Memories of The Four Horsemen
rode through the blood
of these nurturing women
like a vaccination at birth.

With each rhythmic movement
of their short, full bodies
was the economy of appreciation.
A grace which said,
"This day, a gift from God,
we will not take for granted."

A laugh. A good joke.
A mischief without pain.
The joys of life were not wasted
on these wise women.
For them, there was much victory each day
in the evil which did not befall
their families.

For them, "Nothing new,"
from a son-in-law,
meant there would be food again tomorrow
for a daughter—
that their grandchildren were (today)
still all alive
and that no one had been stolen
from his bed last night
to be punished for a crime
he had not committed.

We children were not secure
in the stability of our world.
We were secure only in the love
of the women who mothered us.

Sitting in those long gone theaters,
munching goodies in the dark,
left none of us in doubt
just how much we were loved,
or how much of the family dream
was riding on us.
We were "guilted" with the responsibility
to be the most we were capable of being.
Not just for ourselves,
but for *all* the family
on both sides of the ocean
(on both sides of life).

When a kid pressed his nose
like a hungry porpoise
up to the ticket window in those days
and said his much rehearsed speech,

"One small, please,"
what he got for his ten cents
was a small green ticket
to a fun afternoon
and a whole lot of love
for a lifetime.

Those were good times for America.
Not IN America. But FOR it.
For a country that denied equal rights
to half its population,
and dissuaded an entire portion
of its minorities from voting,
America was the world champion
of the oppressed.

We were defeating the worst enemies
of the free world
and although, in fact,
we were not the home of the free,
we were certainly the home of the brave.
And what is more, we were winners.

In Brooklyn, we had it all.
We were free *and* brave.
It could be seen in our neighborhood.

In those times, on those streets,
Big took care of Little.
It was the credo of the block.
And, oh, what a block!

At the end of World War II,
Manhattan was being squeezed
into the juice of Europe—
a kind of Nedick's blend of the world.

Not so Brooklyn.
Brooklyn was a traditional fruit cocktail!
A Del Monte of the world!
We kept our integrity,
yet we encouraged our commonality.
We were the world, floating in a bowl
the size of one perfect neighborhood.

The country was at war,
but our neighborhood lived in peace.
This was America.

The Pilgrims stepped onto Plymouth Rock
and just took off!
But many of our folks stepped ashore
on Ellis Island,
walked over to Brooklyn
to be near a relative
and never left.

Some never moved to another block!
Everything a person needed
was right there, inside two, three blocks.
Everything. A good place to live.

My world, back then,
was bordered by the movies on one side
and the public school on the other.
In the middle, was the "ball field"
(one magic step off the curb).

On this day, I stopped my reverie
to stand before my old school, P.S. 103.
Hands deep in my raincoat pockets,
I stood on the corner, pencil-straight
like I did on those long-ago autumn days
when the wind turned crisp
and the school rose slow into the morning
like a castle from the moors.
Stiff and formal;
a fortress of emerging civilization
in the middle of our common world
and separate traditions.

Into this institution,
little children,
who were the final dreams
of a lifelong family commitment,
entered either the Boys side
or the Girls side
as Italians or Jews,
Irish and who-knew-what?
And who cared?
All aged six.

They exited six years later,
through the front doors, Americans.

But we didn't think about that—
that was for parents.
We had work to do.

In Brooklyn a kid's work was play.
And it was serious.
We did it better in Brooklyn
than anywhere else in the world.

If it was true that the Air War in Europe
was won on the playing fields of Eton,
then surely, in Brooklyn,
was the developing humanity
which would one day win
a lasting peace in our world.

What a buncha kids we was—
we was da best!
Betcha, chump! Anythin' ya got to lose!
We was da best ever! World class, sure!

The truth was,
that the kids on the streets of Brooklyn
were the most diligent scholars
in the world.
They applied everything
they learned in school to their games.
And later, everything in their games
to their lives.

. . . Standing before the school
that drizzling day in May,
it was like I always felt
when I stood outside St. Patrick's Cathedral.
Intimidated.
It wasn't as big as I remembered,
but it was still scary!

Hell, it, too, was a holy place, sort of.
There, second room on the third floor,
I sat near the window,
behind Sherman who had nits.
He wore a stocking on his head the day
I learned to spell airplane and aeroplane.
And I remember looking out that window
and wondering
(I was always a good brooder)
what in the world I would do
with this new, staggering information.

Well, I didn't do much, I thought,
looking up into that questioning space
of static air as if to answer myself.
Kind of like hitting a fungo,
dropping the bat,
and running to deep center field
for forty years to make the grab myself.
Well, let's see, I mulled,
pounding the pocket of my emotional mitt.
I had parachuted from 104 airplanes.
I flew in enough airplanes
to blacken the sky.
I had an Air Medal from the war.

Hell, it's not like I forgot how to spell
the words airplane and aeroplane,
for chrissake!

But I guess I had disappointed myself
that I really didn't do too much
with the buzzwords of my generation—
didn't launch the Space Age with them,
that's for sure.

Some of the other kids did lots better.

Carl Sagan
was out there somewhere
on those streets as a kid.
I'll bet he looked up from punchball
and daydreamed beyond the clouds
and over the roofs and asked, Why?

Yeah, he did something with
Up and Outer Space.
Aeroplanes, indeed!

And over in Bensonhurst was a kid
named Larry King
who must've stopped
in the middle of Johnny-on-the-pony
to look another kid straight in the eye
and ask, "Are you kiddin' me?"
Yeah, he was always working on
What? and Inner Space.
And besides he had the Brooklyn Dodgers
to think about. What more was there to do?!

Me? I guess I was always looking down
at the spit marks left on the street
to mark my place in the games—
as if the concepts of Time
and Plane Space
could matter to a kid!

It started to rain hard.
I broke away from the school
and took a wide circle to 13th Ave.

Taking a deep breath,
I walked into THE grocery store
of my childhood and of my life.

It was just as it should always be—
always, as before—it simply, Was.
I remember the story of poor Moses
asking God what to call Him
when the children of Israel asked
who had sent him.
And God said unto Moses,
Tell them I AM THAT I AM. (Wow!)
And this grocery store
WAS WHAT IT WAS.
It just WAS.

And it was wonderful.
A bringer of life. A way of life.
Today, as before, it smelled of foods
to nourish families.

Sweet foods which had lived
before they died—
and would live again,
in the strength they gave
to make little legs jump
and big dreams come true!

Sausages and yellow raisins.
Sharp cheeses and smoked salmon.
Turkish candies and Italian oils,
Jewish rye bread and Colombian coffees.

Foods in bins and in cases.
Foods strung from the ceiling
and spilling over from sacks.

Here, were the omnivarious goodies
of the world come to town!

I swallowed the smells
and ingested the sights.
Ah, it was good that here,
human hands touched the food.
Placed it in bags
(marked with quick
crayon glyphs)
only a grandmother could identify
without opening!

And then the flat pencil
from out behind the ear, struck the bag
and ran over all the numbers
like an alien probe. And, Boom!
The entire bill was totaled!

It's probably been a hundred years
since the grocer's pencil made a mistake!
No electronic gear available today
was as quick the grocer's eye.
Who *were* those guys?!

Yeah, from those hands
and out of those bags,
I had been fed as a boy.

When you ate in such celebration,
someone was sure to ask the next day,
"So, whadidya have good to eat?"

In my neighborhood,
they would ask three questions:

"Howse business?"
"Howse the family?"
"So, whadidya have good to eat?"

A guy could get his doctorate
explaining the significance
of those three questions.
A guy could get to be
the university president
explaining the Order
of those three questions.

A guy wouldn't have to explain any of that
to anybody in my neighborhood.
(We all had doctorates, sort of.)

I moved around the store
in a kind of floating suspension;
Captain James T. Kirk,
of the Starship *Enterprise,*
trapped in another dimension,
trying to make contact and get back.

I was surprised when what I said
was answered by the men who ran the store.
Old men with Eastern European accents
asked my grandfather's name
and talked wisely to themselves
in a hushed, quick language
which was many languages.

The one with the wisest eyes of all—
liquid eyes, and sad,
the color of cornsilk,
nodded and made slow faces;
expressions of human emotion
like from an animator's drawings
someone flicked with his thumb
to make a penny movie.

My eyes filled, when he said something
I couldn't quite make out,
but it made me feel seven years old again.
And at home.

I was starting not to feel so good.
(Looking backward is its own kind of dizzy.)

Maybe I should have stayed in Manhattan
with the Vietnam Vets.
That's a kind of "crazy" I understood.
I had to leave . . .

Back outside, the rain had stopped.
I stood still on the corner
trying to remember how to exhale.

The mind is a paranoid creature
which looks both ways for Truth.
On finding none, it looks In.

And I felt a great, rising swell of a truth
gathering from within me. Carrying me with it.
Cruising off my intellectual edges
like a tsunami waiting to dash ashore
and take all before it
to a splintered, inland place of new truth
and modified agreement.
Emotionally, I crested with it.
Physically, I swayed on the street corner
to the rhythm of its rising.
And then it fell in on me.
Crashed over me.
Brought me up
a mile down my soul
a drowning new thing
clinging to this day
as if it were a palm tree.

The dry truth was—
That Life is not a linear experience.
It does not sequentially occur to us
(like falling dominoes)
one flat day at a time.
No. There are levels of knowing.
And many ways to know it.

Science is a way.
And loving, too.
Maybe even Death (no one knows).

There are levels of simultaneous truths
which give the character of a thing
its place and its time;
its meaning and its value.
And all of my life,
ALL of all life was happening
everywhere at once—
to all of us.

The ones who went before
and the ones who are Now,
and most especially,
the ones who *would* be.
ALL AT ONCE.
NOW AND FOREVER.

Oh, shit!
Vietnam and dead babies,
Brooklyn days and Asian nights
happening all at the same time.
Forty years ago and forty years from now,
forty days and forty nights—
it's all desert
and it's all right Now . . .

Cries from the street
brought me "up" from my guts.
The street where I was born
was barricaded with wooden horses
like in a street scene
from a students' uprising in Paris.

Actually,
it was for a "raising up" of students.
These days it was a play street.
Young men, orthodox Jews,
in their early twenties,
leaned on car fenders
and observed the children
like urban shepherds
attentive of their flock.

The boys roller-skated
on the glass-smooth asphalt
with a ferocity and competitiveness
which seemed inconsistent
with the calm demeanor
of the young rabbis
in traditional dress.

I remembered the fierce play
on that street.

And I knew something
about Israeli ground troops
and their ancestor Maccabee raiders.
The street was smooth all right
and so was their blood.
But the street was hard.
And the kids were tough.
The rabbis were serious.
And the games were not play.

I had played different games
in a different time,
but I, too, had been prepared
for the same inevitable struggle.

We, of the old neighborhood
were always prepared for the inevitable.

Darting in and out of the cars,
skating behind the delivery trucks,
we kids of Brooklyn
developed the speed and grace
to zigzag through the cross-fires
of Verdun,
Normandy,
Inchon,
Khe Sanh.

Always it was the street
which prepared us for the mud.

I was standing on the corner
of the street where I was born.
On my side of the street.
I could leave now.
I could keep the memories and walk.

In two hours I would address
many thousands in Manhattan.
I didn't have the time for this.
I wouldn't owe me an explanation
if I just turned around and left.

I walked straight to my house . . .

It was just as before.
I could have closed my eyes
and heard the sounds.
"Ooo-OO! Steeev-ela! Supp-per Tiime!!"
I looked up and that second-story window
from which I was called
from ball games and sword fights.
It was just where it always was.
A window to the world.

But it didn't look real this day.
Once, my mother or my grandmother
would have been up there behind it.
Now, I felt it was only a facade.
If it opened, maybe the whole universe
would be on fire behind it.

I was getting a little nauseous.

The houses on either side
were remodeled duplexes.
Mine was just as it was. It had no color.
Just like the black and white memories
I had of my childhood.

Time as a concept
turned to silt in my head.

The stairs up to the porch
were lined with lion-clawed flowerpots
just as before.
(The sandstone demigods of my play.)
I used to be fascinated
with the cold stone feet of the lions
and would pet them and talk to them
as if the rest of their bodies were there.

Christ, forty years,
and the same flowerpots were still there!
I patted the head of one of the creatures
(that still wasn't there)
and it still felt right.
I was starting to get really nauseous!

My feet started for the top
of the stoop.
Slowly, like when I'd waddle up
with a "load" in my pants.

I could sense through the bottoms of my feet
that on each step of my ascent
up those stairs of my childhood,
the friction was less real—
that movement and record were shuffling.

I felt the concrete steps relax into sand
and the sand become a mix of air and fear.
I went up slowly in the space,
yet I fell backward in the Time . . .

In those days, there were chairs
under the windows where my mother and I
would take the afternoon air.
I have a sense of her reading a book
with one hand while rocking my carriage
with the other.
The air was sweet.

I had no thought of the people
who might live here now.
Not until the old lady peered
from behind the drapes.
She snapped me out of the past
with an expression of terrible alarm.

"I used to live here when I was a boy.
I just came by for a look around."
This, said in a tone and pitch
contrived to speak volumes
of my gentle nature and innocent intent.
(It is difficult to seem what you are.)

She moved from the window—
I went to the front door
hoping she wasn't calling the cops.

She passed from the inner door
to the outer door.
She just stood there,
in that glass-encased, airless,
dead space which allowed us to enter
the home in winter by degrees.
I knew behind that door
Then and Now would merge.

She wore a grandmother's sweater
and a grandmother's shoes.
A shapeless woman of enormous energy
and profound sorrow.
She had eyes like a startled sparrow.
And I loved her like she was my own.

"I kent let you in. I kent let you in!"
she said, in a Yiddish accent so thick,
so rapid, I wasn't sure of her words—
but I was certain of her meaning.

"It's mine grandson
or I vould let you in,"
she said, holding the door
just wide enough to permit me to enter—
as if some "real" monster
would be unable to squeeze in with me.

I moved to protest—
that she shouldn't let me in,
but then I was there, inside, with her.
In that place of deep-breathed limbo
between the cold outside world
and the warm family home.

The last time I was in that vestibule
my grandmother wrapped a scarf
around my face and head
(like I was a mummy)
and told me to walk to school backward
(against the wind).
What lifetime was that?

. . . Twenty years later,
moments before a dawn patrol,
I would walk back inside a straw hut,
sit back down at the wooden table
(with a sigh and a deep breath)
and guiltily return to eat
my unfinished breakfast rice
(just like my grandmother would have wanted—
no wonder we lost the war!)

When I went back outside
to where the troops were waiting,
the sergeant respectfully asked
why I had gone back inside.

Looking up to heaven
(where my grandmother was now pleased)
I properly responded,
as if talking to a retard,
"Because, Sergeant, I want us
to have a good day. That's why."

On that patrol
we killed three old men and a small boy.
From somewhere within me they watched
as the old woman's face before me Now
and my grandmother's Then became one.
"I was born here, nice lady,
We moved when I was seven."

And then I cried. I don't know why.
I just did.
Like maybe, when you're in therapy
or something and you talk about a thing
that you didn't mean to—
and you cry.
And it's all right.

"I know. I know," she said
as if she knew.
I knew she knew.
Before she was a Jewish grandmother
she'd been a Jewish mother,
before that, who knew what?
She knew all right.

And all I could do was cry
and be comforted by this little woman
with the large sweater
who, after a time, led me into her home.
Like I was family.

He was in the kitchen. The Prince.
And the bananas.
The Prince was in his high chair.
The (mashed) bananas were everywhere.
On his face. In his hair,
squishing through his fingers,
sliding down the wall.
Everywhere but in his mouth.

In his mouth there were only protests.
Against bananas. Against high chairs.
Against no ice cream. Against me.

He was the kind of kid
rednecks take to K Mart
just so they can say "no" and spank
for the morning,
while the rest of the world
(shopping in the next aisle)
wonders what the kid's done
and whether to call the cops.
(Damned rednecks.)

I can't shop in K Mart since "the Nam."
Can't bear to hear a child cry.
I've got to wait for a sale at Saks
to get a deal.
Nobody spanks his kid in Saks.
(God'll punish you and make you poor again.)

But the Prince had never been spanked.
And never would be.
The Prince had self-esteem
and a job to do—
find out what's wrong now,
and fix it when he grew up.
I liked him. He was my kind of kid.
A little prick.
He reminded me of me.

I took this in with a glance
as his grandmother fell to her knees
with a wail and a washcloth.

With her free hand
and without looking up, she waved,
"Go. Go. Valk aroun' for a look-see!
Der'es changes, no?"

My feet shuffled me away
with a milk-horse mentality—
they knew the route—
I was just along for the ride.

I wasn't surprised at all
that the first stop
would be at the end of the hallway,
just past the kitchen.
It was a large walk-in closet today,
but it didn't used to be.
During the war years, this room
was the sanctuary of survival.

I stood there, arms dead at my sides,
in the open mouth
of what had been simply, profoundly,
the pantry.

A wide-open, floor-to-ceiling cavern,
devoted to food.
Cans and jars, boxes and cartons—
all shapes, all sizes—
stocked for all appetites in stacks.
Shelf upon shelf.

In the old days it had stood ready
like for an open wall-locker
inspection. Always right.

This World War II, rationed family
had been combat ready!
We stored and hoarded, bartered
and cajoled for the children.
Mothers and grandmothers
ate sparingly from it
and gave generously.

Yet, there wasn't any love
in the pantry. I remembered that.
In the pantry there was only war.
A real war. Against poverty.
And hard times.

It existed like an ammunition dump
at the far end of the house.
Revered. Distant. Often inspected.
And not a little feared.

The love that came with the food
was added in the kitchen—
as the food was cooking.
As the food was being served.
As the meal was being shared.

In those days the real "living room"
was the kitchen.
And the kitchen table was the altar
for the life experience.
To pull up a chair at supper time,
was to sit together
in a kind of worship.
It was a special time
when the events of a harried or boring
business day could be reconstructed
as a joyful adventure.

A time when conversations
and confrontations could be reworked
to allow the family members
to feel good about themselves.
Good enough to go back again, tomorrow.
As they always did.
To earn more food for the pantry.

Sometimes, as a boy,
I would be sent from the kitchen
on a mission to the pantry.
This was a big deal to a little kid.
A bag of egg noodles
or a jar of peach preserves.

Had this been the pantry
of my Italian grandmother
(a few blocks away)
I would have been sent for a salami
or some rotini pasta
(an equally solemn occasion,
but when completed,
the cause of less celebration).
A nod or a tousling of hair was praise.

And I would stand, once in a while,
in this cathedral of a room,
and ponder the condition
of the "starving kids in Europe."
The ones I would hear about so often
at mealtime.

And I would wonder
with all of my child-wonder
how much of this magnificent room's food
a starving child my age could eat
all at once.
Would he even believe his eyes
in such a room as this?

I decided a starving kid
could eat it all.
Starting with the graham crackers.
(Which is where I would have started.)
And next, the applesauce.

Geeze, how lucky to be a starving kid
and get to eat all you wanted.
I was abstractly envious.
And wondered if I would one day
meet one of those kids.
I decided, yes,
and that we'd eat Mallomars for a week
and play war.

Wait.
I had that thought before.
It had not been forty years
since I remembered thinking that.

And suddenly I was there at the edge.
Wrestling on the ledge of "then" and "now"
like Holmes and Moriarty on the precipice—
and we fell—
over and down.
Plunging through the perfect past
tumbling into the cold, thinning dead past
to stop dead—
dangling on the sheer face
of outer wall memory—
suspended twenty years up—
by the seat of my reality
stuck on an outcropping of a well-rooted moment
of pantry and war
of madness and survival . . .

. . . Twenty years before,
in the back country of another continent,
I sat in a handwoven chair
sharing a corner of an adobe
with a chameleon—
just him and me
hiding as best we could
(his complexion more effective than my camouflage).

The sun, two fingers from the horizon;
two flesh eaters
waiting for the "killing time"—
always a personal time beyond thought—
a neutral, instinctive time,
when immediate motive and transcending dream
meet in a soulful silence
to say their last good-byes.
The man-warrior and the lizard-hunter
were allies in our separate intentions;
friends from within our common natures.

This day, within hours,
one or both of us
could be dead.
If not, others (strangers to us)
would be dead.
I do not know in what deliberation
or reptilian trance the chameleon waited.
I brooded over a CARE-package goody
and tried to think of nothing.

That night I was going to attempt to infiltrate
a jungle insanity that separated villagers
from food and their enemies from humanity.
I was playing war for keeps.
People were starving.

I was eating a Mallomar.
And "puff"—
I was standing in the pantry
in the middle of a daydream
just like now I was standing in the pantry
in the middle of the same daydream.
Oh, God.

That day, in the bush, when the sun set,
I tossed a cookie at the chameleon
and waved a perverse "Happy Hunting!"
from the door
like some big-titted Swedish girl
in a 1950s nudist film.

Next morning I came back and he was gone.
Maybe like the five Viet Cong
I had met on the trail were gone.
Or maybe, like me,
he was just still hunting.

. . . I could hear the Prince screaming
for ice-cream from the kitchen.
I moved into the main body of the house.
Christ, it was like entering a museum
after dark.
And I felt it should have been guarded.

That it *was* guarded.
By what, I wasn't sure,
but I really felt unsettled, observed.
It was me, watching me.
Making certain I did not take away
(or break) any of this room's treasures.
Look. Touch. But do not move a memory.

I could feel myself fall into play—
a "huckle-buckle-who's-got-the-buckle"
kind of game.
The clapping got louder and louder
the closer I got to feeling
like the "little me" again.

Shit. What was I doing here.
I was a poet, for chrissake—
I was due to perform in a fucking hour or two
and I was here in Brooklyn,
in an old house I hadn't been in
for forty years, with an old lady
I could hardly understand
and a brat kid who wouldn't stop crying.

And here I am tiptoeing around
in the back bedrooms of a stranger's home
looking for memories from World War II
on the Day that New York
was welcoming us home
from the Vietnam War.
Great timing, schmuck!

Oh shit, I was stressed out!
Out of Time, out of Place.
And yet, how could I be?
This stuff was IN me. Always.
IT WAS me.
Oh shit, I was fucked.

. . . There was the window
that looked out to Johnny's house.
My friend.
A real tough. First one I ever knew.
Johnny only played marbles
for "keepsies."
Spent the four years I knew him
wearing pants with precisely
the same hole in the left knee.
Didn't make a difference which pair,
always the same hole.

The kid was a study in "tough."
Used to have a permanently runny nose.
Like some big kids
would throw their heads back
to make a curl behave,
Johnny used to curl up his lip
and suck the snot back up his nose.

What a kid!
Johnny was my first hero.
He taught me how to talk mean
and look bad.
At least he tried.

Later, much later,
I could do those necessary things.
But as a kid I was a failure.
Even with the nose thing.

Johnny could do it, sure.
But he used to get colds.
He was *supposed* to get colds.
He was a goy (whatever that was).
Me? I got allergies.
You only got colds
if you didn't eat right or dress right.

I tried that runny-nose routine,
and instead of that wet trail of life
which ran down the manly gutter
from under Johnny's heroic nose,
all I got was a yellow bubble
the size of Mars on my upper lip.
It looked terrible
and made my eyes water.

Johnny was so neat. He said neat things.
"Up your hole with a Mel-O-Rol.
Up your ass with a piece of glass."
What a guy!

I'd practice all that stuff
in front of my grandmother's mirror
and it somehow never worked for me.
Where *was* that mirror?

I stood in the master bedroom
of this stranger's home
and moved a fancy chair away
from the vanity table
so I could be at exactly the right place
in this room where I would practice
my tough-guy speeches
in that three-way mirror.
(Beam me up, Scotty!)

Once a day, after school,
I'd stand there for a few minutes
looking at myself from all directions
(all I hadda do was move my eyes)
to get a feel for the true impact
of my ferocity.

One afternoon,
I was practicing really ugly faces
before I went outside to use 'em
on Johnny.

"Dirty Jew! Mockie bastard!"
(snarl, snarl.)
Holding a really menacing look,
I scanned the three mirrors with my eyes—
I had to admit this was the best yet!

I looked pretty scary
for a seven-year-old kid
who had a hay-fever attack at lunchtime
and had eyes swollen
the size of manhole covers.

About that time,
my mother sticks her head in
between the slightly opened
glass doors.
"Sweet Stephen, when you're finished
in there, I have something special
I'd like to tell you."

At the kitchen table,
I licked the cream from the wrapper
of my Yankee Doodles when she told me
she was Jewish.
I just looked at her kind of funny.
Like for the first time.

Outside, the rest of the day,
I just sort of walked around, you know?
Not gettin' into anything.
Just workin' on it.

I didn't know how a person
could be two things
at the same time.
How could she be Jewish
AND be my mother?

And besides, what was Jewish?
I was too embarrassed to sleep.
And a little angry, too.
Heck,
that was the meanest I ever was so far.
And I'd never get to show Johnny, now.
He wouldn'ta believed it!

Several weeks later,
I was in front of the mirror again.
I was really gettin' good now—
that's for sure.
"Dirty WOP! Dago—somabitch! Greaseball!"
Great stuff (with my ugly faces).

Couple a minutes later,
here comes my grandmother.
She's got a plate
with my favorite on it!
Thick sliced black pumpernickel bread
with rich creamery butter an inch thick
and sliced again into five "fingers"
so's a guy could pick up one at a time.
Mmmm.

Sitting on the bed, bouncing and humming
while I ate my bread, I listened vaguely
(and then, intently)
as my grandmother told me that my father,
and therefore me, too, was Italian.

Oh God! Not that!
I mean what did a kid have to be?
Everything?
For chrissake.
Can't a guy call a guy some names.
Shoot!
It was all I could do to finish
my bread. (almost.)
She also told me I was an American
and that was like bein' everybody
all at once.

It was really tough
bein' a bad guy in Brooklyn.
Everybody was everything!

. . . Truly, I thought
as I reminisced in that back room,
in my whole life since I left Brooklyn
as a boy of seven,
I never met a gook or a nigger or a spic.
Or an Anything.

I didn't like many people since Nam.
In fact, distrusted almost everybody.
But that was always because of "who" they were.
Never because of "what."

And my first, best friend, Johnny,
was killed in Vietnam.

I found his name on "The Wall"
by accident at the dedication in '84.
Story was, he got shot in that left knee of his
and didn't have the sense to stay down.
Just kept comin' and comin'.
Tough guy.
Got the silver star. Posthumously.
They buried him in a new uniform
and I betcha—
betcha anytin' ya got ta lose, chump—
ya could dig him up tamorrow
and there'd be a hole in the left pant knee.
Tough guy.

. . . Back in the kitchen,
The Prince was protesting the spoon
of strained pears poised precariously,
in front of his pursed lips
by his grandmother's left hand.
I recognized it was the left hand
immediately.

Why not?
The left hand was the "heart arm."
The one they always used on us
to "guilt" us.
It was the one
if you didn't eat from quickly
when they held it out to you,
could give 'em a heart attack.

Great message.
Eat or kill your grandmother.

I wonder if anywhere, at any time,
one of those kitchen bullies
with the huge breasts
and the smothering hugs
ever did just keel over and die?

You know, just held out her arm
until the kid's face turned blue
and the old lady's turned white.
And she just dropped.

Boy, I'll bet *that* kid was sorry!!
Poor Grandma.
Shiit!

It was in that posture then,
with her arm outstretched—
the cuff pulled above her wrist—
that I noticed it.
The purple tattoo on her forearm.
And *my* heart stopped.

Here, right next to the pantry
of my childhood,
was one of the starving kids of Europe.
And worse.
Oh my God. The concentration camps.
Oh, God . . .

She looked up as I reentered the room.
I sensed she had seen that "look" before.
That expression on a stranger's face
of pity and of revulsion.

Smiling warmly, she rubbed her arm
slowly, like it was an orphaned child.
She added a nod to the brave motion
which seemed to say, "Yes it's true,
but life goes on—and we must live it."

She never lowered the spoon
from the Prince's mouth.
And I wanted to strangle the little shit.
My eyes brimmed
and I shook my head a little
(like I was Steinbeck's Lenny)
and sat heavily into a chair.

I was in a kind of numbed stupor—
a profound disorientation.
Too much life for one day.
Yesterday and today crowded my reason.
I was truly, dizzy.
I wanted to leave,
but I felt like a seven-year-old.
Where could I go?

She began singing—
cooing, really, a folksong.
Russian maybe.
The Prince was steadfast.
It was like I wasn't there.
She was giving me the room
to be miserable.

I looked back up to her.
Seated, I was at eye level with her arm.
Her tattoo appeared blurred through my tears,
and somehow I was focused
on the second digit; the seven.

I studied it as from a great distance—
it swam like a magnified protozoa
in the liquid of my eyes.

I felt of it.
Disappeared and descended into it;
a preverse kind of target fixation.

It had a kind of wiggle
like a tadpole's tail.
And I wondered of that monstrous moment
of indefinable pain
and untranslatable shame,
at what child-pulling of her hand
against the Nazi's needle
had caused that twist
on something twisted—
like a venereal wart
on the flesh of a rapist's inadequacy.

I looked away
as the arm began a slow chugging
toward the tunnel of the Prince's mouth.

"Choo-choo—open-vide!
Here comes da choo-choo!
Whoo! Whoo!! Wheeee!"

The tunnel stayed closed.
I was definitely gonna kill
this little stinker!

Sometime later, over tea,
(boy, was I late)
while "Sweet Boy" napped
in banana-faced, ice-cream dreams,
the old lady,
who I began to realize was not old, told me,

". . . I vos a small girl. Vun of twins.
Mengele, the Angel of Death,
(something, something in Yiddish)
selected us personally.
He used us for experiments,
(something more in Yiddish)."

No saliva graced my throat.
I suffered paroxysms of dry-swallowing
and sat there, too ill even to choke.

". . . In the beginning," she continued,
"there vos no roof on Auschwitz
and very little water to drink."

". . . black clouds vould gather
and the children vould huddle together.
And vait. And vhen the rains came
we vould open our mouths
vide as ve could
and close our eyes.

"I vould shield mine eyes mit mine hands
so to see my sister drink—
such joy! to vatch raindrops dancing,
dancing, dancing on her tongue!"

She told me of many things
but none more significant than her accounts
of the human compassion shown her
by some ordinary German citizens
when later she toiled in forced labor.

That she could articulate
even one gesture of humanity
from the bowels of such contempt
for the dignity of all life,
was like watching
the fiddler on the roof
dance on the lip of my teacup.

She did not tell me,
nor did I ask,
but I sensed that her sister
was not as strong as she.

I started to tell her things
about myself and our family,
but it was too late for that.

And my tears at our good-bye
went unnoticed by her
as she too, was now unfocused—
was elsewhere, in another time.

We wobbled at the door
as if some mad projectionist
was running the film backward and forward.
We were out of synch,
each in a space of our own.
We said nothing.
Our hands groped for each other.

And as I left the home where I was born
a couple of wars before,
the rain fell straight and steady
on the streets where I had played.

And I stopped halfway up the block
to open my mouth to heaven and to drink.
And the raindrops did not dance on my tongue.
Nor in my soul.

I walked like I'd forgotten how
and descended from Brooklyn
into the chthonic world of the BMT.
The real, real, New York Now.

Outside the subway car,
on the way back to Manhattan,
the subterranean world
of dark and dirty timelessness
matched my mood.

Inside the car,
the flat paint of the Transit Authority
fought with the inks and crayons
of nameless, faceless vandals.
A serpentine, linear battle of half-wits—
the "No" vs. "Yes" struggle
of rebellion against establishment
for the graffiti title
of the underworld.

The Black Madonna face
of Miss Subways 1985
commanded a position of honor
at the front of the car.
It graced the vulgar muraled scene
with a mustachioed serenity.

The mispelled promises
of explicit sexual favors
scribbled on her forehead
seemed to contort her impassive smile
into warm obscenity.

Her poster
was a microcosm of the conflict in the car;
maybe of the world.

Somewhere, in this,
a real statement about social confusion
and basic human needs run aground—underground.

Somewhere,
in what seemed to be adolescent mischief
below the grasp of authority,
were the primitive,
almost Cro-Magnon drawings
of a section of American society
trying to explain its anguish
with sex and government.

Here, the concept of Love
(on the Madonna's face)
and the vandal's need
(to control that love)
in the FUCK FUCK FUCK
violent rape of beauty,
was a conflict too involved
for a veteran on this special day
of Homecoming.

But still, there was much of this visit
to answer . . .

I sat alone in that crowded car
swaying to the rhythm of the tracks
like a solitary Bronsonesque figure
with a five hundred-dollar raincoat over my suit
and a two-bit sneer on my face
and invited no company . . .

What was it about my childhood
that got me to this middle-aged upheaval?

Brooklyn was long before Vietnam.
All American men my age
suffered the bad luck and ill-timing
of drawing Vietnam and women's lib
in the same ten years!

Sort of like getting hit by a truck
the same day they told you
about the stomach cancer.

Sure, we were prepared for a world
that no longer existed.
Sure, we were this nation's
last generation of heroes—
unburied dinosaurs,
extinct only in our lack of purpose.

Our nation would honor us
(if only it could) posthumously.
It ignored us instead.

But that had nothing to do
with the message of Brooklyn.
Or the message I would share
an hour from now in Manhattan.

Brooklyn, too, was about love and war.
But it was more.
It was, I felt, but could not reason,
was about peace as well.

Somehow, in Brooklyn's indefinable
condition of social acceptance—
of identity and mutual respect
for separate ways,
there was a human climate
conducive to cooperation.

A commitment to survival.
And to new beginnings.

There was something
in that place of many people
that took on the character
of one person. A good one.

In that bright thought
(quick as a tunnel opens)
I changed my mind for the day
and my purpose for a lifetime.

On the way to speak of war
(to men who had fought one)
I decided to speak instead of peace
(which none of us have ever known).

On that day, May 7, 1985,
I became a warrior for peace.
Because I was born in Brooklyn
and in my heart
would stay there—
a human being.

The Prince and I have work to do. . . .

PORTRAIT OF A MAN
for Glen Williams

Out there,
beyond the pull of man's imagination,
at such distance to betray the concept of "near"—
on days safe from the nails of earthly calendar,
on nights so long as there is grief and dream,
in the vastness, then, between what is known
and what is surmised,
the whisperings of midnight, self-prophesy,
speak to the ear of each man
the truth of his essential nightmare—
that he, accountable for the life he has led,
will die. And forever be dead.

We, who can, move indoors to warm illusion
and the certain lie by which all else is denied.
For the moment, we are safe in separate myths.
But not so all of us.

I know a man whose time is near.
A man who is innocent of the life
you and I have led.
And yet, this night,
while we frolic, he dies.

He stands alone, arms at his side,
beneath the shadow of his god
and says with his undeniable
(almost) will to live,
"Please, and with respect,
when you've finished dancing,
I'd like to live, thank you."

He dies from unseen wounds
drawn deep into his blood
from a long gone war
too much discussed
to be so misunderstood.

He was awarded no Purple Heart
for the cancerous time bomb
which has imploded in his guts
and in his bones and not in his heart
which beats the deepest, basest rhythm
that courage and sacrifice can play.

LiveandLove LiveandLove LiveandLove.
It is the rataplan of the innocent
and of the brave.

This man is my friend and I love him.
And I do not know how to help.
And for that, I am a little angry
and a lot sad.

It seems we do not know the world
through which we pass
We only come to recognize the surface
of what we do not know.
What is familiar we call known.
What remains unknown we claim by faith.
Psychology and mythology are the ruling dyad
of the inside, outside world of the unknown.

In the physical world of experience,
we are comfortable in the proximity
of what does not threaten to kill us.
In such places we build our homes.
In such people we place our trust.

Often we are wrong.
As my friend was wrong . . .

He was as young as you and I when he was born.
He trusted his mother and smiled up at her.
She put him up for adoption.

He trusted his country as did you and I.
It sent him to Vietnam—way up in I Corps.
They deny that Agent Orange is killing him.

He trusted his second wife (just like we did).
And loved her daughter as if she were his own.
His wife left after the chemotherapy began.

I've never spoken to my friend about his God.
I'm sure he trusts Him like you and I do.

My friend had other friends, but no one visits.
My friend had fellow workers when he could work.

A doctor recommended that he call the Vietnam Vets.
And so my friend told me on a ferryboat ride
that now he has lots of brothers and a real family.

And I cried. And I'm still crying.
And the more I can't help him, the angrier I get,
and the more I remember my friend saying,

. . . "Just tell them I said to keep pluggin' away
and to keep workin' for peace. That's all there is.
Make it safe for the children. Tell them for me."

SOMEWHERE, A WOMAN

We dare not sleep
(our dreams will steal our breath)

We dare not war
(our bombs will steal our time)

The gods count our money
(the kings spend our children)

Nothing can save us
(but our women, whom we despise)

Please, somewhere, a woman.
Anywhere, a mother.
Forgive us. Take charge.

We need courage now
(and survival without profit)

Only the heart and mind of woman
can save this world
from the systems
of man kind.

IN VICTORY OR DEFEAT

From any nation
each man
returning from war
stands alone in the rubble
of his personal Homecoming.

In victory or defeat,
his former life has collapsed
under the undeniable weight
of debunked values.
His cultural upbringing is in ruins.

He enters a world of his own creation.

The institutions
of education and government,
marriage, marketplace and church
have been kicked out—
one "flying buttress" at a time,
until the whole of it collapsed
under his rude questioning.

Each new man
sifts the smoldering ruin
of his former life
for some uncharred thing of value—
some remnant truth
he can salvage—
that he can hold up
(still warm to the touch)
and say, "With this, I begin again."

This generation of world veterans
has seen combat on four continents
(in more than a hundred shooting wars).

What kind of mind could remember them all?
What mother could forget one son?

Hundreds of millions
of men under arms
have killed millions
of men, women
and little children
with nails and clubs,
bullets and bombs.

They did it and continue to do it
in the name of gods,
for the sake of governments
and in the cause of nationalism.
But especially they do it
for the thousand nameless men
who control the world of business
and have not yet found the profit
in peace.

But mostly veterans went to war
because boy children are taught
to say, "yes." For no reason at all.

Drafted, recruited,
impressed, conscripted
heroes and cowards
and all of us who just made it—
sick, lame, lazy, half-near dead
and almost crazy
(and worst of all, untouched by it all)
all come home to question
why they fought,
for whom they fought
and the true identity of the real enemy.

The absolute worst off,
the most lonely of all—
those for whom homecoming was easy—
are those who fought a war where they lived;
those morally anguished world veterans
for whom the bodies on the ground
(and the ones which can't be found)
belonged to family, and to friends
and to a thousand well-known lives
undecorated by monument or meaning.

For a time, most veterans turn inward—
"one man" awareness patrols
searching for a truth to believe in
(which will not die laughing at him).

On all sides of the issues
on both sides of any ocean,
veterans mistrust anyone in a position to lie;
Wives, girlfriends, government officials,
salesmen, lawyers, and the rich.

Veterans trust dogs,
children under twelve,
masturbation,
the chair facing the door
and any weapon in the dark.

Some read, some can't
some hate, some don't.
All agree—no matter what the war
no matter what the cost of victory or defeat,
war as a solution to economics
or as a perpetuation of social justice, fails.

Each senses that military victory
cannot conquer human nature.

A failed government is a system
which does not allow people to be people.
War topples the government
and kills the people;
it replaces things, but changes nothing.

Veterans are people who believe
that peace is government
which will accommodate nature.

Paratrooper or terrorist
infantryman or medic—
armor, air, or artillery—
guerrilla fighter or
counterinsurgent,
each man reborn in combat,

who has a child
or a wife,
each who has a dream or a job
a rage or a sorrow—
once having seen war,
wants only for his country
and his world to be at peace.

Throughout the world,
translated from every language,
the new veteran dances to the same tune:

"Stosh, you bum,
when you gonna work?
You gonna lie around
the rest of your life, or what?"

"Chan, you child of deception,
since the border war
you only empty your rice bowl—
you never fill it."

"Jorge, you are not the only man
with one leg in this province.
Others do not spend their days brooding."

"Myron, you schmuck,
I told you to be an accountant
and war or no war,
now, that you're back,
you're going to be an accountant!"

"Lutuli, if you continue to go
from village to village
speaking as you do,
surely, they will come for you."

"Vladimir was a strong man.
The strongest of us all.
He was the last we thought
would take his own life . . ."

Although no person need go to war
to commit to peace,
it is the collective conscience
of the worldwide veteran community
which speaks most positively about peace.

It is the refusal of these men and women
to give up the hope and the responsibility
for the future of their children,
which gives the world its finest hope.

If there is a weapon to be deployed
against war, and against prejudice,
it is these men and women of our veterans.

If there is a tool with which to shape
meaningful cooperation among governments,
if there is a way to the natural trust
and equality of the sexes
(without which there can be no world peace)
it is these men and women of our veterans.

These warriors for peace,
are the combined forces of recruitment
of reason and resolve on this planet.
Their Homecoming is to our one and only world.

These brave men and women
whose loyalty is to all our children—
it is with them we begin again.